FIRST 50 CHORDS
YOU SHOULD PLAY ON PIANO

by Alistair Watson

ISBN 978-1-70514-249-3

HAL•LEONARD®

Visit Hal Leonard Online at
www.halleonard.com

World headquarters, contact:
Hal Leonard
7777 West Bluemound Road
Milwaukee, WI 53213
Email: info@halleonard.com

In Europe, contact:
Hal Leonard Europe Limited
1 Red Place
London, W1K 6PL
Email: info@halleonardeurope.com

In Australia, contact:
Hal Leonard Australia Pty. Ltd.
4 Lentara Court
Cheltenham, Victoria, 3192 Australia
Email: info@halleonard.com.au

CONTENTS

Introduction 4

The Basics of Reading Piano Chords 6

Major Chords (White Keys).......................................9

Minor Chords (White Keys)......................................12

The Black Keys 15

Major Chords (White and Black Keys) 16

Minor Chords (White and Black Keys) 20

More Major Chords (White and Black Keys)..............24

More Minor Chords (White and Black Keys)..............31

Seventh Chords 36

Dominant Seventh Chords 37

Major Seventh Chords..44

Diminished Seventh Chords......................................49

Suspended Fourth Chords 52

Minor Seventh Chords...57

INTRODUCTION

Welcome to *First 50 Chords You Should Play on Piano*. Throughout this book, you will find some of the most popular and most often used piano chords. If you can't read music, there's no need to worry. We've included keyboard and hand diagrams as well as chord symbols on every page, showing you exactly how to play each chord on the piano keyboard. We've also included a popular-song excerpt after each chord, so you can start playing music straight away. Every song progresses systematically, allowing you to combine each new chord with those previously learned. You'll love being able to apply your skills straight away, playing great songs with the chords you can hear in famous recordings.

If you have no experience of music theory, we've also included essential information on the basics of reading and playing piano chords. It's right at the start of this book so you'll be good to go in no time! To play the piano safely and comfortably, make sure that you observe the following.

Sitting at the Piano

- Sit tall and lean slightly forward, balancing your body weight on the front half of the piano bench.

- Keep your feet flat on the floor.

- Adjust the bench height so that your forearm is parallel to the floor and your fingertips are touching the surface of the keys.

Hand Position

Let your arms hang relaxed at your sides. Notice how your hands stay gently curved. Keep your hands relaxed and curved as you raise them to the piano keyboard. When you are playing the piano, keep your fingers in this relaxed, curved position.

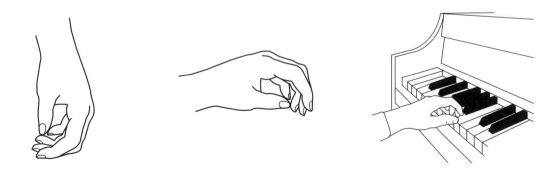

We've organized the chords into several different categories:

Major Chords (White Keys): These will be the "happy" sounding chords. Major chords are made up of three notes called a **triad**. This group of chords only uses the white keys on the piano.

Minor Chords (White Keys): These will be the "sad" sounding chords. They are also made up of three notes, but in this case one of the notes is lowered in comparison to a major chord, creating a minor interval. Again, these chords use only white piano keys.

Major Chords (White and Black Keys): These "happy" sounding chords use a combination of white keys and the thinner, black keys. They still consist of just three notes.

Minor Chords (White and Black Keys): These "sad" sounding chords also use a combination of white and black keys on the piano keyboard. Again, they still only use three notes.

Dominant Seventh Chords: These chords consist of four notes and have lots of energy. They make the music sound like it wants to move on and are especially popular in jazz and blues music.

Major Seventh Chords: These chords have a "sweet" sound to them and are used frequently in jazz and pop. They also consist of four notes.

Diminished Seventh Chords: These four-note chords sound really tense and are used across pop, jazz, and film music to create a sense of drama and uncertainty.

Suspended Fourth Chords: These are three-note chords and are used in many of the great pop hits. Two of the notes are closer together than in an ordinary triad and they are used to create a sense of longing in songs.

Minor Seventh Chords: These chords maintain the "sad" sound of a minor triad but have more color owing to an additional, fourth note.

There are a lot more than just 50 chords to learn on the piano, but this will give you a great start!

THE BASICS OF
READING PIANO CHORDS

Keyboard Geography

- The piano keyboard consists of white and black keys. The black keys are arranged in groups of twos and threes.

- The white keys for the note "C" lie immediately to the left of the two black-key groups. The middle-most of these keys is called "middle C."

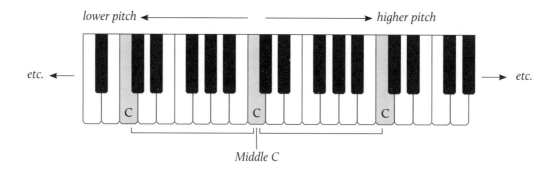

Middle C

The Musical Alphabet

- Musical notes get their name from the musical alphabet, which has seven letters: A, B, C, D, E, F, and G. This sequence repeats up and down the piano keyboard.

- Starting at "middle C," find all the Cs up and down the keyboard. Notice how they sound the same (i.e., they are all higher and lower versions of the "same note").

- Now do the same with Ds, Es, and the rest of the musical alphabet.

The Staff

- Music is notated on a pattern of five lines and four spaces called the **staff** or **stave**. Notes are printed either on the lines or in the spaces between.

- In the left-hand margin of each line, we have a clef: the **treble clef** (mostly for right-hand playing) and the **bass clef** (mostly for left-hand playing). The clef determines the letter names of the notes on the lines and spaces.

Treble Clef

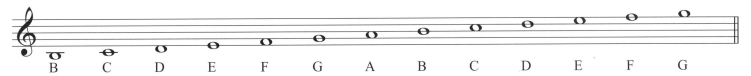

B C D E F G A B C D E F G

Bass Clef

F G A B C D E F G A B C D

Middle C

- Middle C is on its very own, short line called a **ledger line**. (Although the two notes below look different, they are exactly the same note.)

- Look at the following group of treble-clef notes. Work out where they are on the piano keyboard and play them with your **right hand**. If you start with your thumb on middle C, you should end up with your little finger on the G in the following line of music.

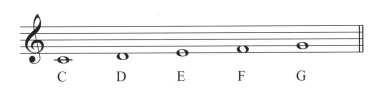

C D E F G

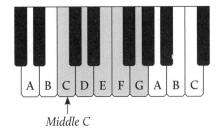

Middle C

- Look at the following group of bass-clef notes. Work out where they are on the piano keyboard and play them with your **left hand**. If you start with your thumb on middle C, you should end up with your little finger on the F in the following line of music.

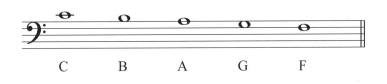

C B A G F

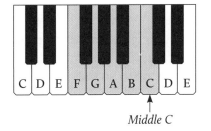

Middle C

Finger Numbers

- Each finger is assigned a number. Finger numbers usually appear above and below the musical notes.

- In this book, recommended fingering is shown on the keyboard diagrams for ease of reading.

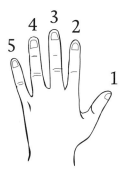

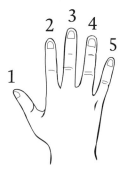

Reading Piano Chords

- Most of the chords you will learn in this book consist of three notes (called a triad).

- Piano chords are represented by an uppercase letter. This book will show you what notes are in each chord in notation format and on the piano keyboard.

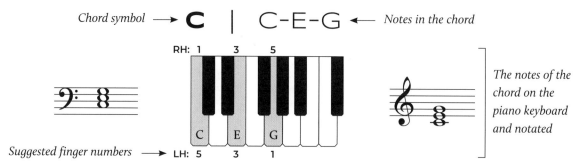

- We'll also show you different ways of playing the same chord through **slash chords**. You can see from the example below that a slash chord has all the same notes as its original, only in a different order. The letter after the slash tells you which note is on the bottom of the chord.

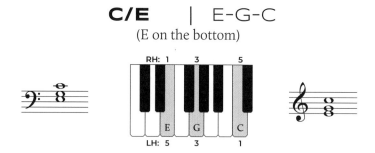

Playing the Songs

- Each new chord comes with a popular-song excerpt, allowing you to apply what you've learned straight away.

- Every song progresses systematically, featuring both the chord you've just learned and those previously encountered. These chords are all as you hear them on famous recordings, so you'll enjoy being able to play along in no time!

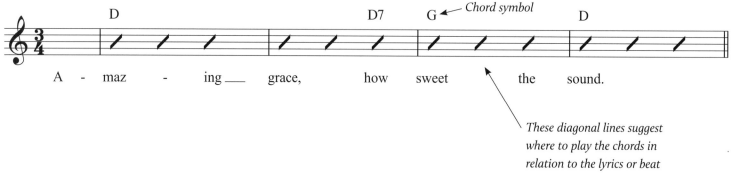

MAJOR CHORDS
(WHITE KEYS)

C MAJOR

C | C-E-G

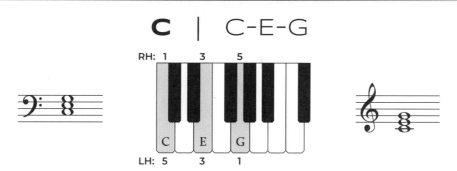

There are two further positions of this chord:

C/E | E-G-C
(E on the bottom)

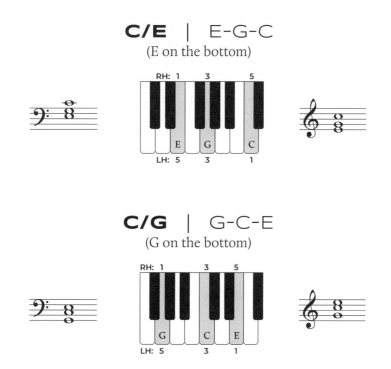

C/G | G-C-E
(G on the bottom)

FRÈRE JACQUES (ARE YOU SLEEPING?)
Traditional

Frè - re Jac - ques, Frè - re Jac - ques, dor - mez vous, dor - mez vous?

Son-nez les ma - ti - nes, son-nez les ma - ti - nes. Ding, dang, dong. Ding, dang, dong.

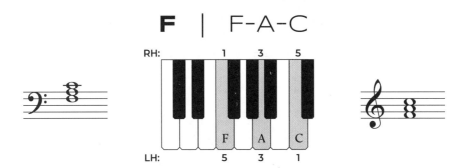

F | F-A-C

There are two further positions of this chord:

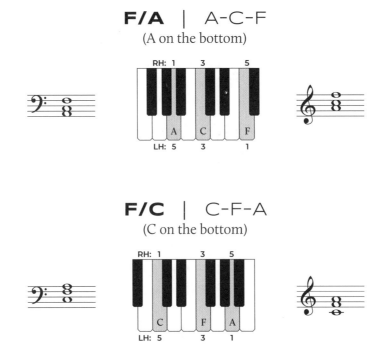

F/A | A-C-F
(A on the bottom)

F/C | C-F-A
(C on the bottom)

STREETS OF LAREDO
Words and Music by Marty Robbins

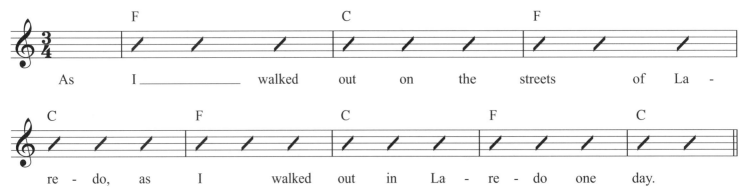

As I _____ walked out on the streets of La-

re - do, as I walked out in La - re - do one day.

G | G-B-D

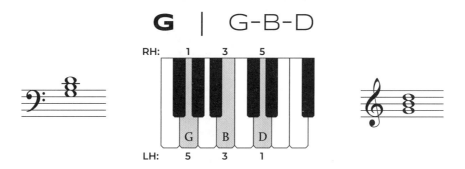

There are two further positions of this chord:

G/B | B-D-G
(B on the bottom)

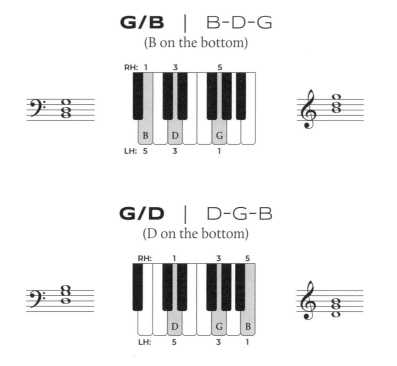

G/D | D-G-B
(D on the bottom)

TWIST AND SHOUT
Words and Music by Bert Russell and Phil Medley

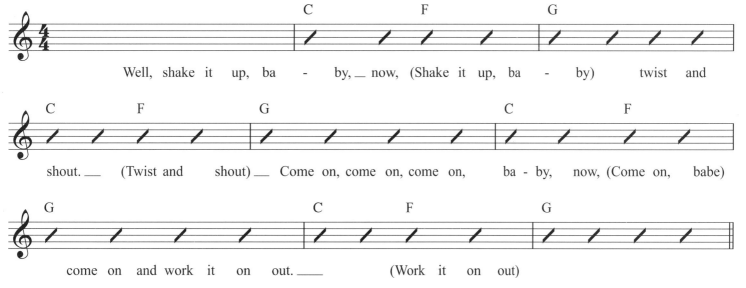

MINOR CHORDS
(WHITE KEYS)

D MINOR

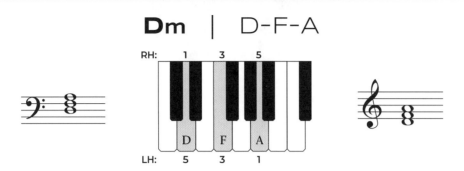

Dm | D-F-A

There are two further positions of this chord:

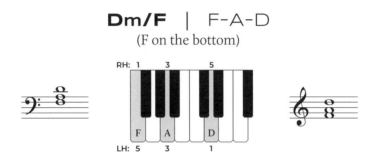

Dm/F | F-A-D
(F on the bottom)

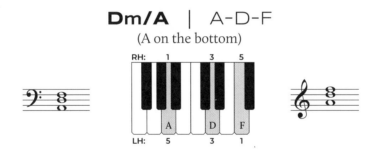

Dm/A | A-D-F
(A on the bottom)

SCARBOROUGH FAIR
Traditional English

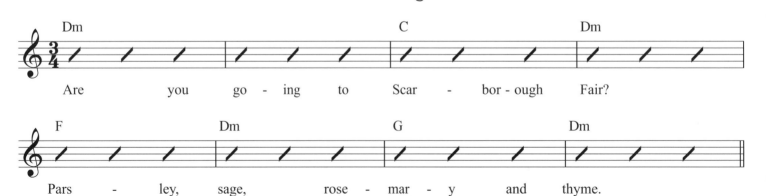

Dm

Are you go - ing to Scar - bor - ough Fair?

F   Dm   G   Dm

Pars - ley, sage, rose - mar - y and thyme.

Em | E-G-B

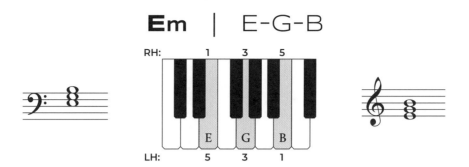

There are two further positions of this chord:

Em/G | G-B-E
(G on the bottom)

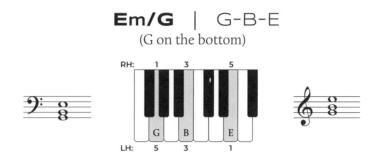

Em/B | B-E-G
(B on the bottom)

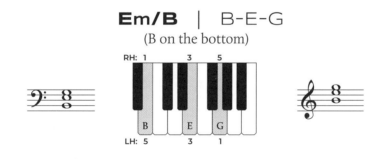

LEAN ON ME
Words and Music by Bill Withers

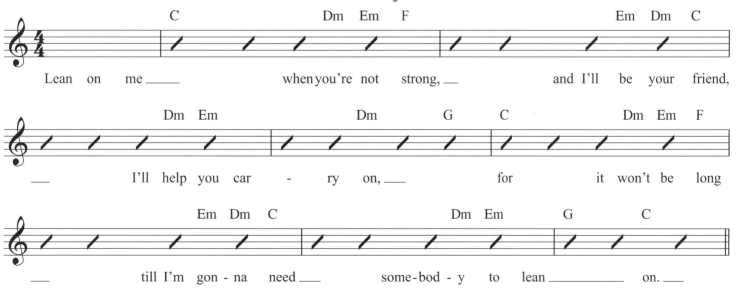

Am | A-C-E

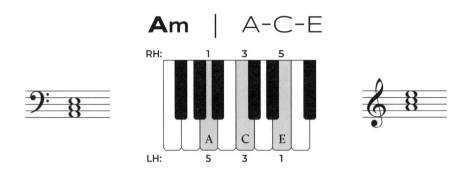

There are two further positions of this chord:

Am/C | C-E-A
(C on the bottom)

Am/E | E-A-C
(E on the bottom)

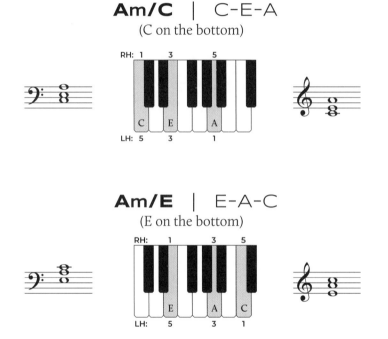

COUNT ON ME
Words and Music by Bruno Mars, Ari Levine and Philip Lawrence

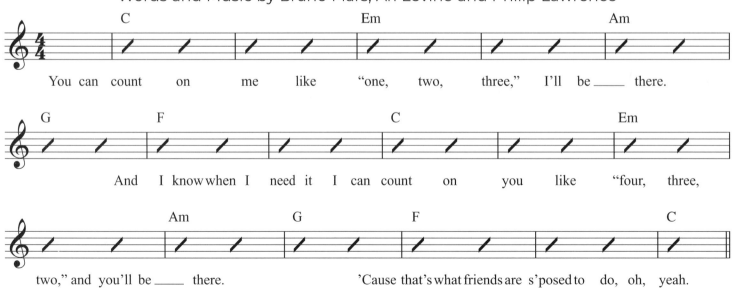

You can count on me like "one, two, three," I'll be _____ there.

And I know when I need it I can count on you like "four, three,

two," and you'll be _____ there. 'Cause that's what friends are s'posed to do, oh, yeah.

THE BLACK KEYS

The black keys are called either sharps or flats, depending on what chord you're playing.

A **sharp** sign (#) indicates a **half step higher** (up to the right).

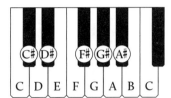

Practice finding sharps up and down the keyboard.

This is a natural sign. It means go back to playing the white "C" key.

A **flat** sign (♭) indicates a **half step lower** (down to the left).

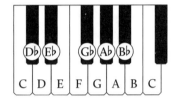

Practice finding flats up and down the keyboard.

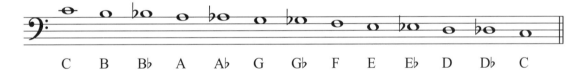

You will then notice that all black keys can have two possible names. For example, an F♯ is exactly the same black key as a G♭.

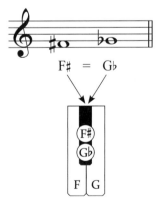

From now on, the chords you play will involve playing black keys (sharps and flats). Even ordinary major and minor chords will need sharps or flats, depending on where you are on the keyboard. For example, if you want to play the chord of D major, you will need to play the black F♯ key as well as the white D and A keys.

MAJOR CHORDS
(WHITE AND BLACK KEYS)

D MAJOR

D | D-F#-A

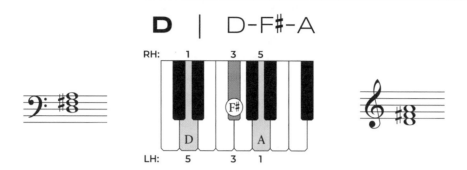

There are two further positions of this chord:

D/F# | F#-A-D
(F# on the bottom)

D/A | A-D-F#
(A on the bottom)

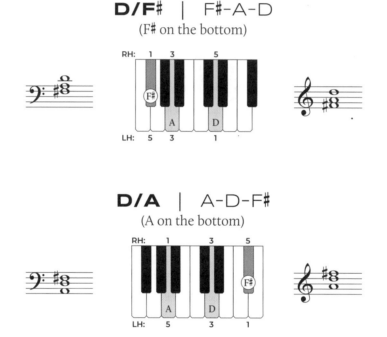

MAN IN THE MIRROR
Words and Music by Glen Ballard and Siedah Garrett

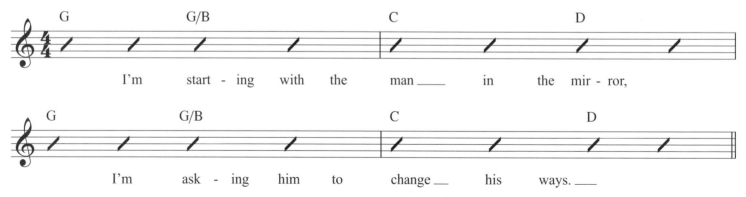

I'm start-ing with the man ___ in the mir-ror,

I'm ask-ing him to change __ his ways. __

A | A-C♯-E

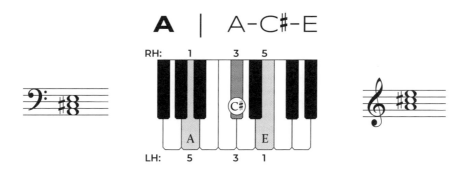

There are two further positions of this chord:

A/C♯ | C♯-E-A
(C♯ on the bottom)

A/E | E-A-C♯
(E on the bottom)

SUMMER OF '69
Words and Music by Bryan Adams and Jim Vallance

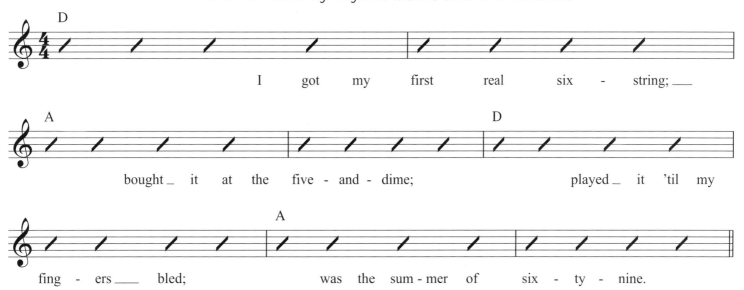

I got my first real six - string; __ bought __ it at the five - and - dime; played __ it 'til my fing - ers __ bled; was the sum - mer of six - ty - nine.

E | E-G#-B

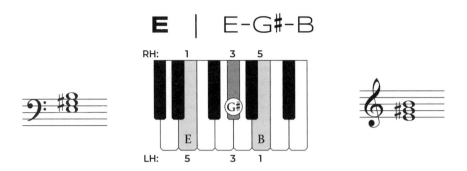

There are two further positions of this chord:

E/G# | G#-B-E
(G# on the bottom)

E/B | B-E-G#
(B on the bottom)

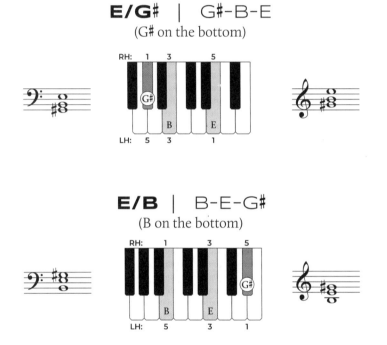

HEY JOE
Words and Music by Billy Roberts

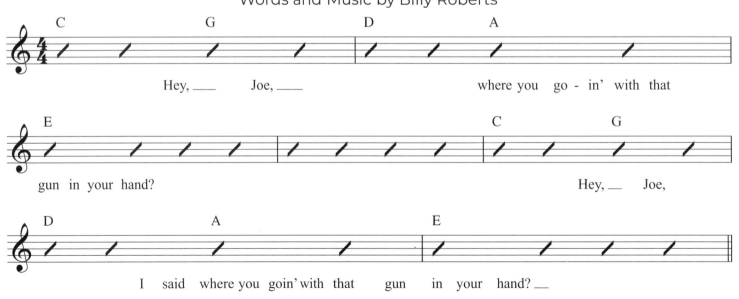

Hey, ___ Joe, ___ where you go - in' with that gun in your hand? Hey, ___ Joe,

I said where you goin' with that gun in your hand? ___

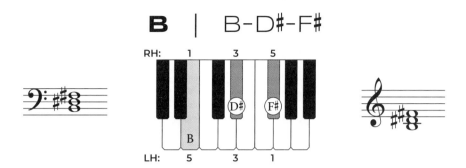

B | B–D♯–F♯

There are two further positions of this chord:

B/D♯ | D♯–F♯–B
(D♯ on the bottom)

B/F♯ | F♯–B–D♯
(F♯ on the bottom)

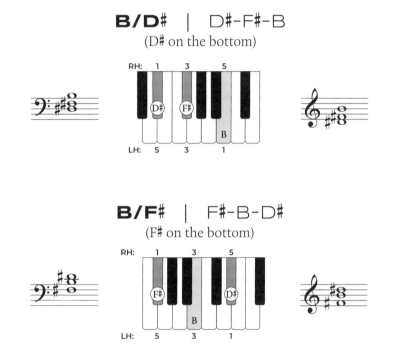

(SITTIN' ON) THE DOCK OF THE BAY
Words and Music by Steve Cropper and Otis Redding

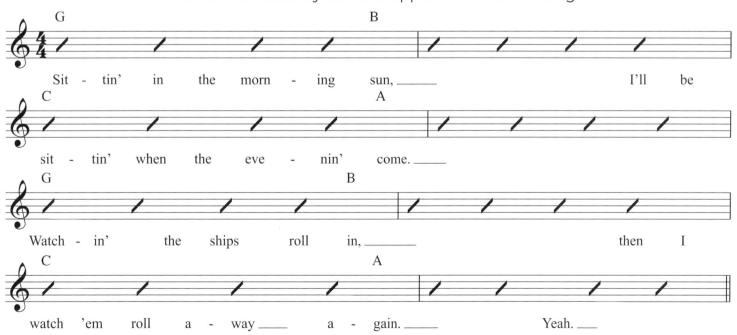

G   B
Sit - tin' in the morn - ing sun, _____   I'll be

C   A
sit - tin' when the eve - nin' come. _____

G   B
Watch - in' the ships roll in, _____   then I

C   A
watch 'em roll a - way _____ a - gain. _____   Yeah. _____

MINOR CHORDS
(WHITE AND BLACK KEYS)

B MINOR

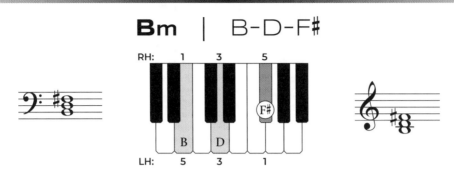

Bm | B-D-F#

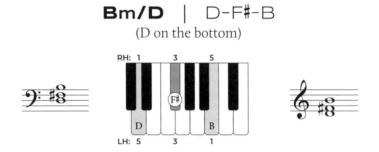

There are two further positions of this chord:

Bm/D | D-F#-B
(D on the bottom)

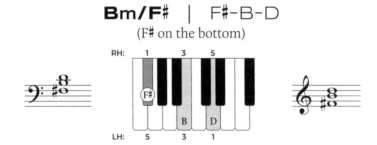

Bm/F# | F#-B-D
(F# on the bottom)

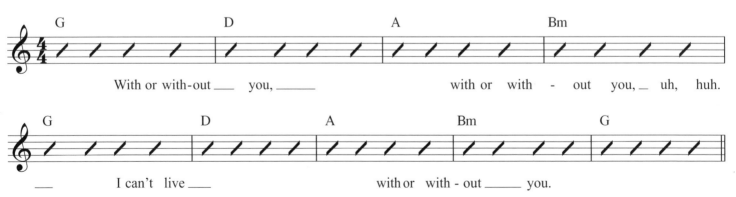

WITH OR WITHOUT YOU
Words and Music by U2

| G | D | A | Bm |

With or with-out ___ you, _____ with or with - out you, ___ uh, huh.

| G | D | A | Bm | G |

___ I can't live ___ with or with - out _____ you.

Fm | F–A♭–C

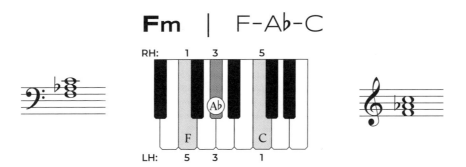

There are two further positions of this chord:

Fm/A♭ | A♭–C–F
(A♭ on the bottom)

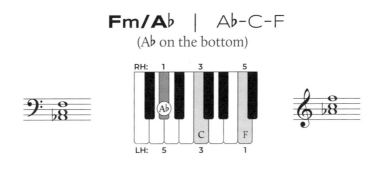

Fm/C | C–F–A♭
(C on the bottom)

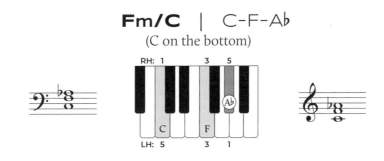

SPACE ODDITY
Words and Music by David Bowie

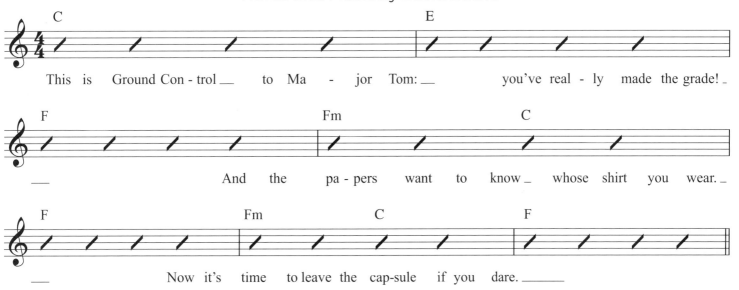

Cm | C–E♭–G

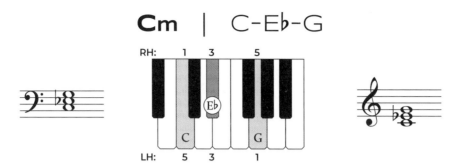

There are two further positions of this chord:

Cm/E♭ | E♭–G–C
(E♭ on the bottom)

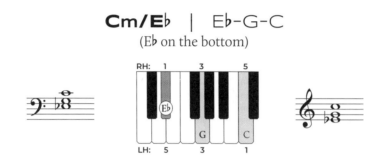

Cm/G | G–C–E♭
(G on the bottom)

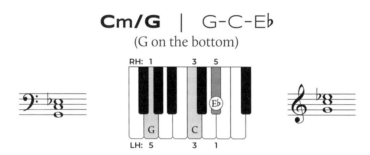

WE DON'T TALK ABOUT BRUNO
from ENCANTO
Music and Lyrics by Lin-Manuel Miranda

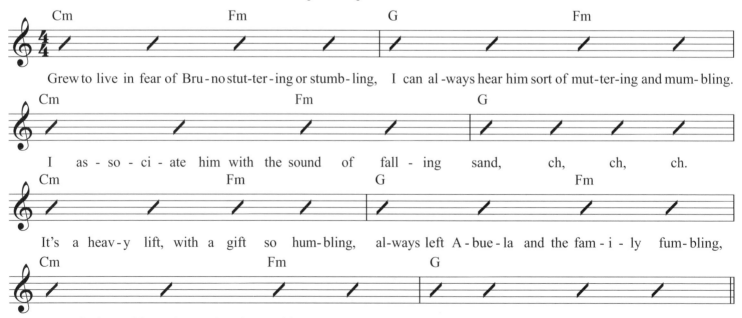

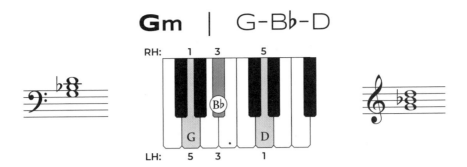

Gm | G-Bb-D

There are two further positions of this chord:

Gm/Bb | Bb-D-G
(Bb on the bottom)

Gm/D | D-G-Bb
(D on the bottom)

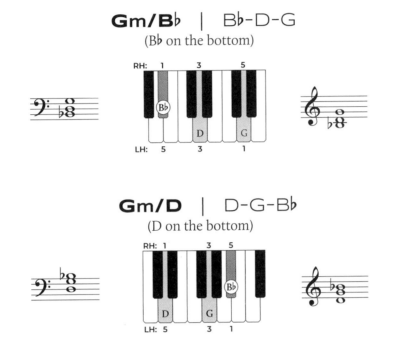

I MISS YOU
Words and Music by Adele Adkins and Paul Epworth

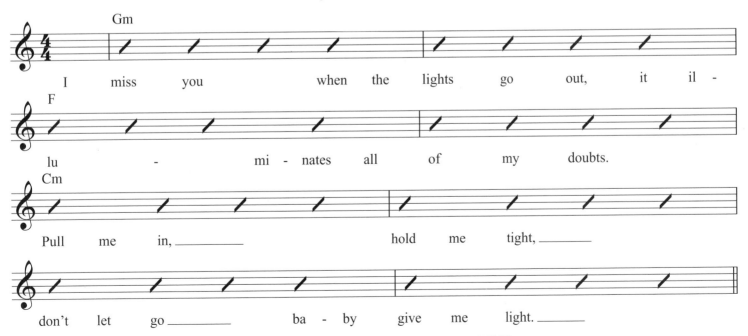

Gm

I miss you when the lights go out, it il-

F

lu - mi - nates all of my doubts.

Cm

Pull me in, _____ hold me tight, _____

don't let go _____ ba - by give me light. _____

23

MORE MAJOR CHORDS
(WHITE AND BLACK KEYS)

B♭ MAJOR

B♭ | B♭-D-F

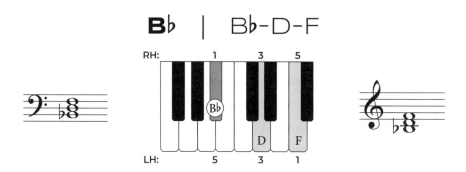

There are two further positions of this chord:

B♭/D | D-F-B♭
(D on the bottom)

B♭/F | F-B♭-D
(F on the bottom)

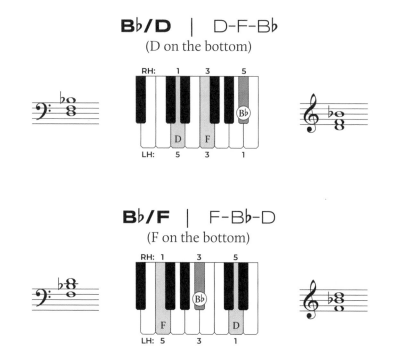

SHOTGUN
Words and Music by George Barnett, Joel Laslett Pott and Fred Gibson

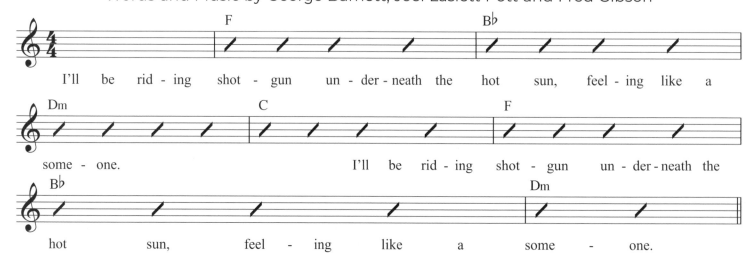

I'll be rid-ing shot-gun un-der-neath the hot sun, feel-ing like a some-one. I'll be rid-ing shot-gun un-der-neath the hot sun, feel-ing like a some-one.

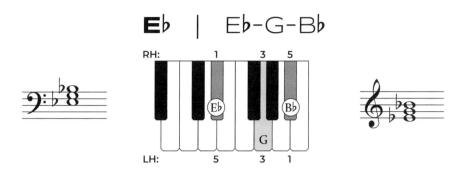

There are two further positions of this chord:

SEE YOU AGAIN
from FURIOUS 7
Words and Music by Cameron Thomaz, Charlie Puth, Justin Franks, Andrew Cedar, Dann Hume, Josh Hardy and Phoebe Cockburn

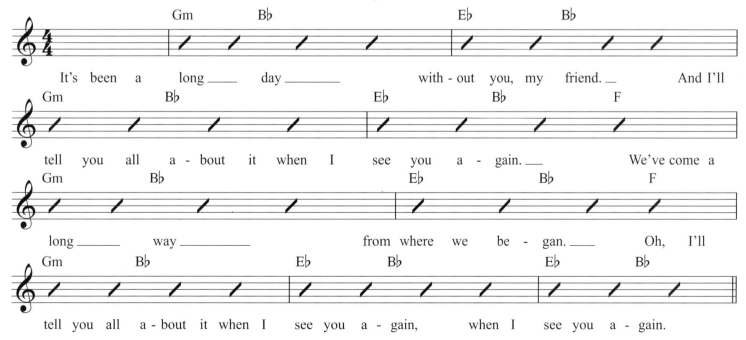

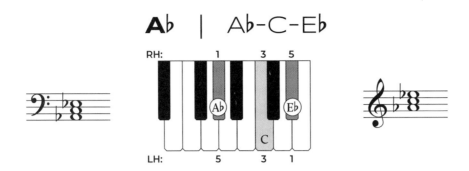

A♭ | A♭-C-E♭

There are two further positions of this chord:

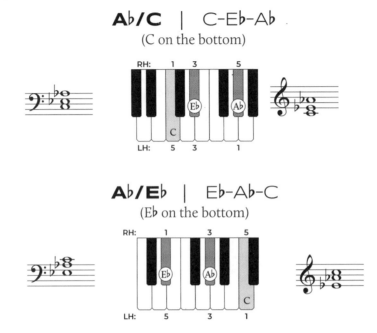

A♭/C | C-E♭-A♭
(C on the bottom)

A♭/E♭ | E♭-A♭-C
(E♭ on the bottom)

GANGSTA'S PARADISE
from the Motion Picture DANGEROUS MINDS
Words and Music by Stevie Wonder, Doug Rasheed, Artis Ivey and Larry Sanders

A♭   Fm   G   Cm

Been spend - ing most _ their lives _ liv - ing in the gang - sta's par - a - dise. _

A♭   Fm   G   Cm

Been spend - ing most _ their lives _ liv - ing in the gang - sta's par - a - dise. _

A♭   Fm   G   Cm

Keep spend - ing most _ our lives _ liv - ing in the gang - sta's par - a - dise. _

A♭   Fm   G   Cm

Keep spend - ing most _ our lives _ liv - ing in the gang - sta's par - a - dise.

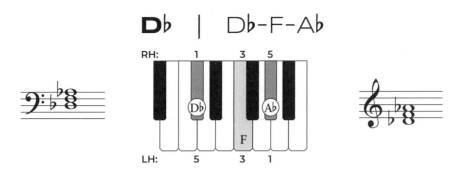

There are two further positions of this chord:

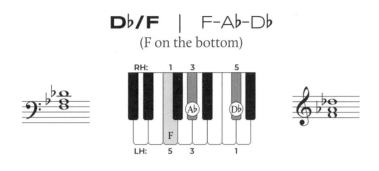

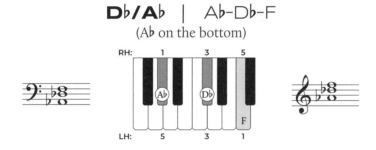

HELLO
Words and Music by Adele Adkins and Greg Kurstin

Hel - lo from the oth - er side. _____ I
must have called a thou - sand times _____ to tell you _____
_____ I'm sor - ry _____ for ev - 'ry - thing that I've done, _____ but when I call _____
_____ you nev - er seem to be home. _____

F# | F#-A#-C#

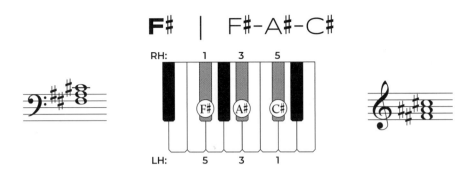

There are two further positions of this chord:

F#/A# | A#-C#-F#
(A# on the bottom)

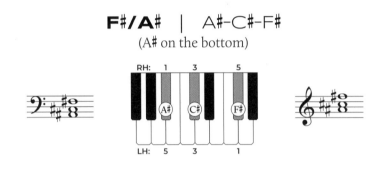

F#/C# | C#-F#-A#
(C# on the bottom)

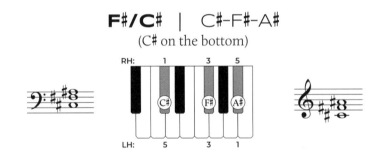

SWEET CAROLINE
Words and Music by Neil Diamond

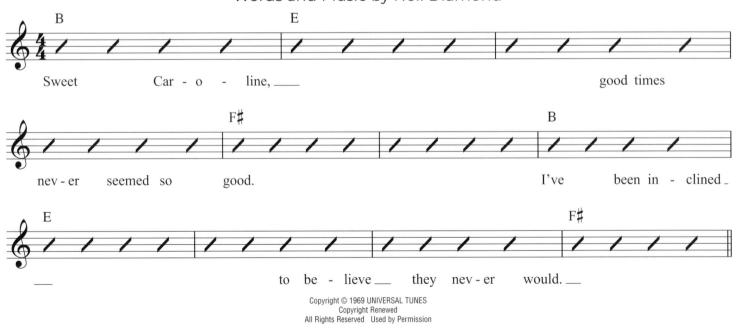

Sweet Car - o - line, ___ good times nev - er seemed so good. I've been in - clined ___ to be - lieve ___ they nev - er would. ___

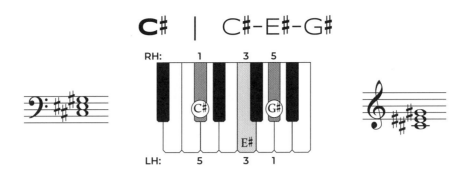

C# | C#-E#-G#

There are two further positions of this chord:

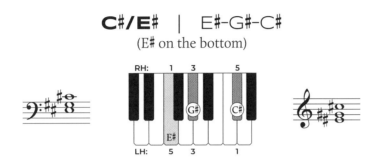

C#/E# | E#-G#-C#
(E# on the bottom)

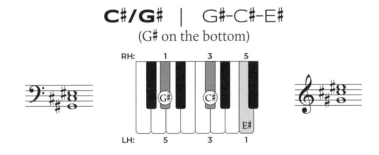

C#/G# | G#-C#-E#
(G# on the bottom)

YELLOW SUBMARINE
Words and Music by John Lennon and Paul McCartney

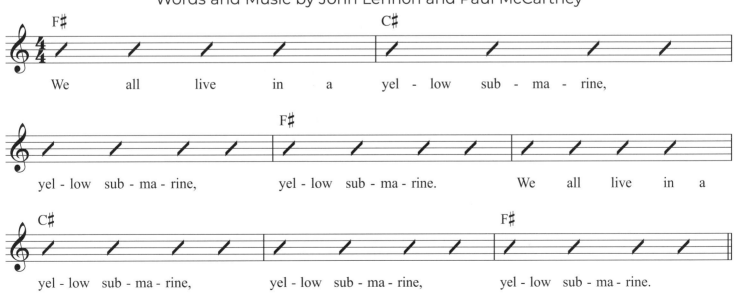

F#   C#

We all live in a yel - low sub - ma - rine,

yel - low sub - ma - rine,   F#   yel - low sub - ma - rine.   We all live in a

C#   yel - low sub - ma - rine,   yel - low sub - ma - rine,   F#   yel - low sub - ma - rine.

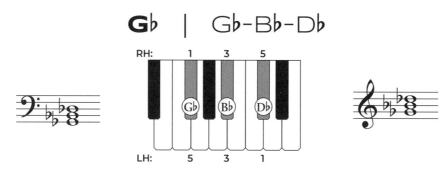

G♭ | G♭–B♭–D♭

There are two further positions of this chord:

G♭/B♭ | B♭–D♭–G♭
(B♭ on the bottom)

G♭/D♭ | D♭–G♭–B♭
(D♭ on the bottom)

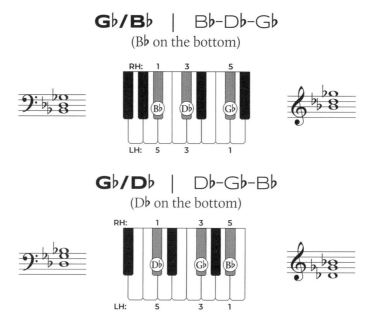

(EVERYTHING I DO) I DO IT FOR YOU
from the Motion Picture ROBIN HOOD: PRINCE OF THIEVES
Words and Music by Bryan Adams, R.J. Lange and Michael Kamen

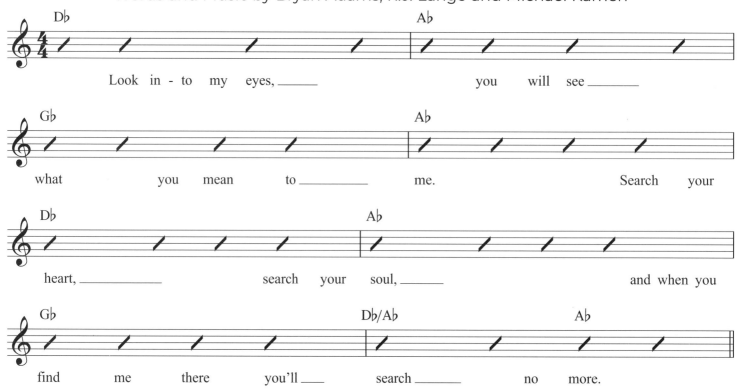

D♭   A♭

Look in-to my eyes, _____   you will see _____

G♭   A♭

what you mean to _____ me.   Search your

D♭   A♭

heart, _____ search your soul, _____ and when you

G♭   D♭/A♭   A♭

find me there you'll ___ search _____ no more.

MORE MINOR CHORDS
(WHITE AND BLACK KEYS)

F# MINOR

F♯m | F♯-A-C♯

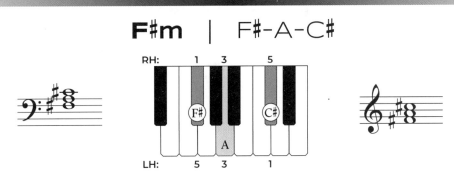

There are two further positions of this chord:

F♯m/A | A-C♯-F♯

(A on the bottom)

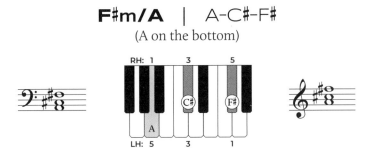

F♯m/C♯ | C♯-F♯-A

(C♯ on the bottom)

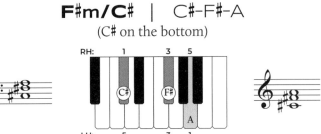

SOMEONE LIKE YOU
Words and Music by Adele Adkins and Dan Wilson

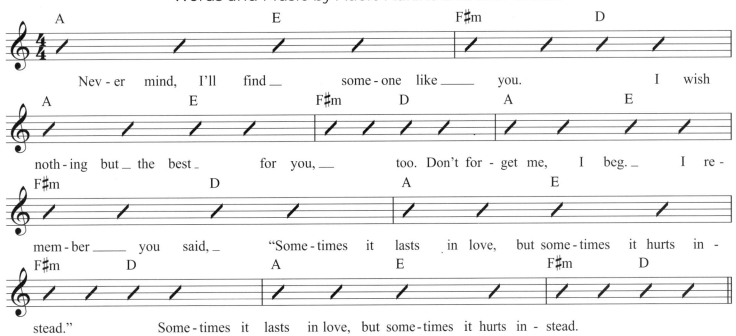

C#m | C#-E-G#

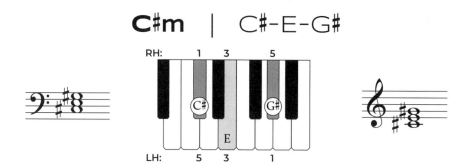

There are two further positions of this chord:

C#m/E | E-G#-C#
(E on the bottom)

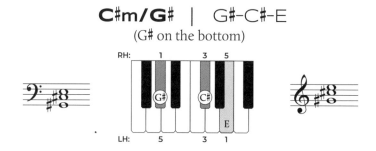

C#m/G# | G#-C#-E
(G# on the bottom)

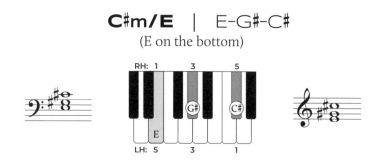

SO WHAT
Words and Music by Alecia Moore, Max Martin and Shellback

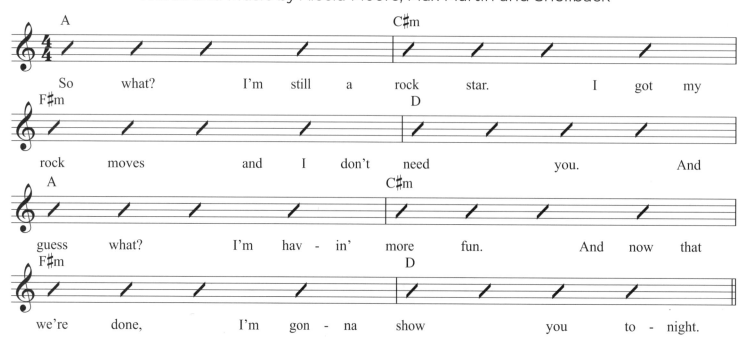

G♯m | G♯-B-D♯

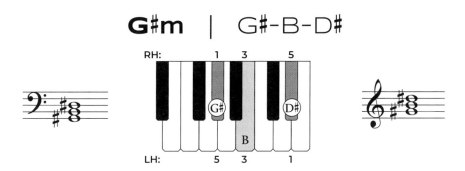

There are two further positions of this chord:

G♯m/B | B-D♯-G♯
B on the bottom)

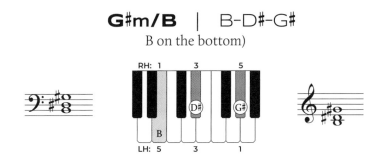

G♯m/D♯ | D♯-G♯-B
(D♯ on the bottom)

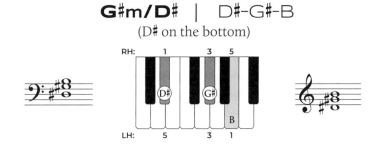

POKER FACE
Words and Music by Stefani Germanotta and RedOne

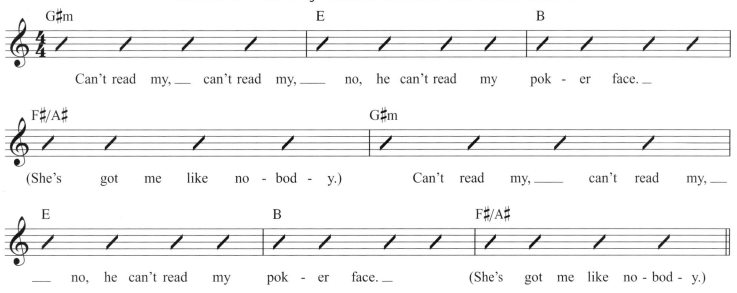

G♯m   E   B

Can't read my, __ can't read my, __ no, he can't read my pok - er face. __

F♯/A♯   G♯m

(She's got me like no - bod - y.)   Can't read my, __ can't read my, __

E   B   F♯/A♯

__ no, he can't read my pok - er face. __   (She's got me like no - bod - y.)

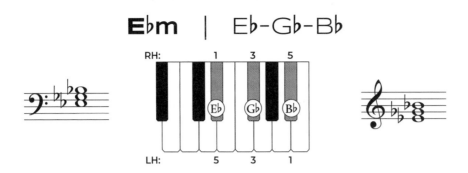

Ebm | Eb–Gb–Bb

There are two further positions of this chord:

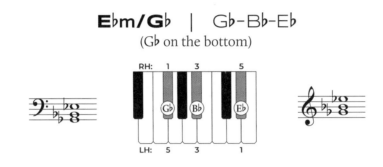

Ebm/Gb | Gb–Bb–Eb
(Gb on the bottom)

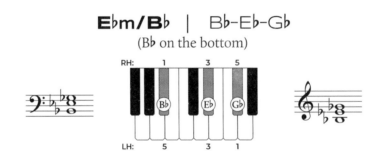

Ebm/Bb | Bb–Eb–Gb
(Bb on the bottom)

STRONGER

Words and Music by Thomas Bangalter, Guy-Manuel De Homem-Christo,
Edwin Birdsong and Kanye West

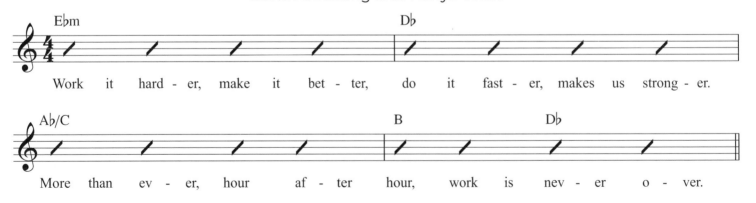

Work it hard - er, make it bet - ter, do it fast - er, makes us strong - er.

More than ev - er, hour af - ter hour, work is nev - er o - ver.

B♭m | B♭-D♭-F

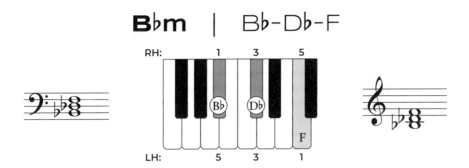

There are two further positions of this chord:

B♭m/D♭ | D♭-F-B♭
(D♭ on the bottom)

B♭m/F | F-B♭-D♭
(F on the bottom)

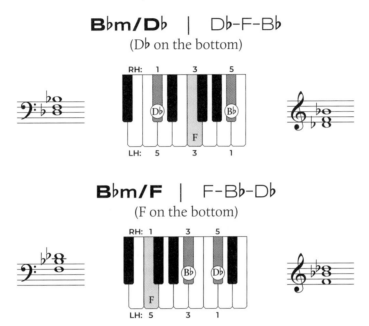

UMBRELLA
Words and Music by Shawn Carter, Thaddis L. Harrell,
Christopher Stewart and Terius Nash

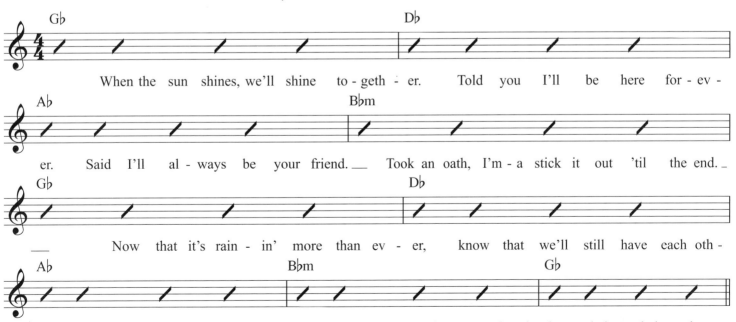

G♭   D♭

When the sun shines, we'll shine to-geth-er.   Told you I'll be here for-ev-

A♭   B♭m

er.   Said I'll al-ways be your friend. __ Took an oath, I'm-a stick it out 'til the end. __

G♭   D♭

__ Now that it's rain-in' more than ev-er,   know that we'll still have each oth-

A♭   B♭m   G♭

er. You can stand un-der my um-br-el-la. You can stand un-der my um-br-el-la, el-la, el-la, eh.

SEVENTH CHORDS

Now, we are going to play some chords that contain four notes. These are called seventh chords and there are several different kinds.

1. A **dominant seventh chord** takes a major triad and adds a note above. This extra note is the seventh.

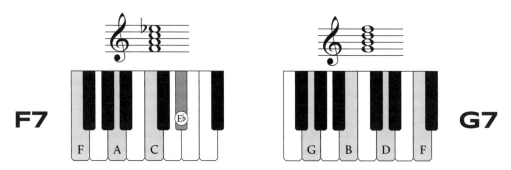

2. A **major seventh chord** is the same as a dominant seventh, except that the added seventh note is raised by one half step.

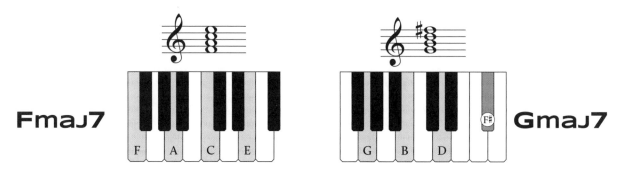

3. A **diminished seventh chord** consists of four notes that, when stacked, are the exact same distance from one another. They don't belong to a particular key, so each diminished seventh is named after the note upon which it is built.

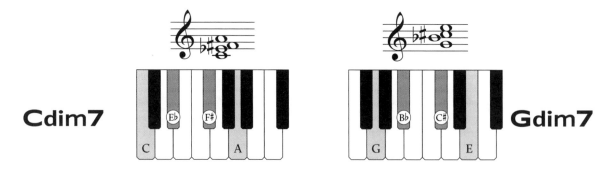

4. A **minor seventh chord** takes a minor triad and adds the seventh note above.

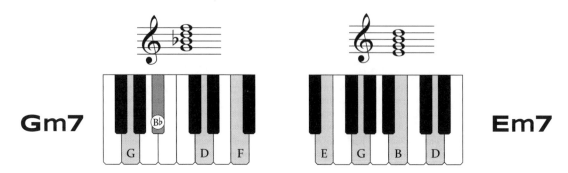

DOMINANT SEVENTH CHORDS
C DOMINANT SEVENTH

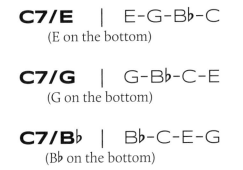

C7 | C-E-G-B♭

There are three further positions of this chord:

C7/E | E-G-B♭-C
(E on the bottom)

C7/G | G-B♭-C-E
(G on the bottom)

C7/B♭ | B♭-C-E-G
(B♭ on the bottom)

BABY LOVE
Words and Music by Brian Holland, Edward Holland Jr. and Lamont Dozier

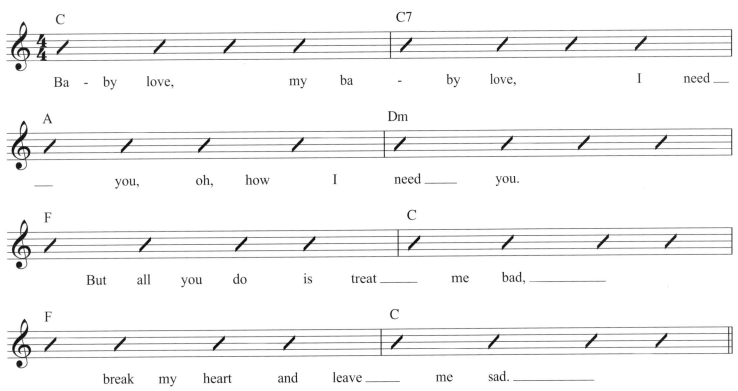

G7 | G-B-D-F

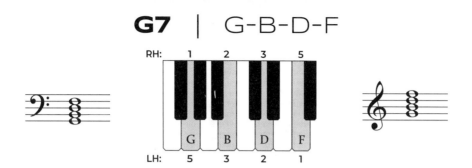

There are three further positions of this chord:

G7/B | B-D-F-G
(B on the bottom)

G7/D | D-F-G-B
(D on the bottom)

G7/F | F-G-B-D
(F on the bottom)

WHAT I GOT
Words and Music by Brad Nowell, Eric Wilson, Floyd Gaugh and Lindon Roberts

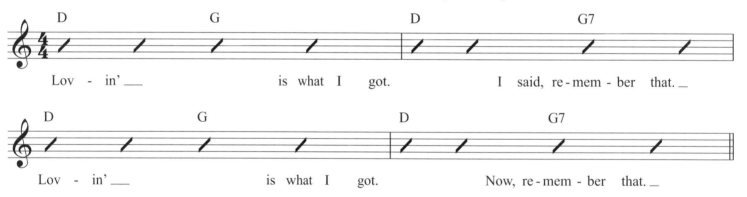

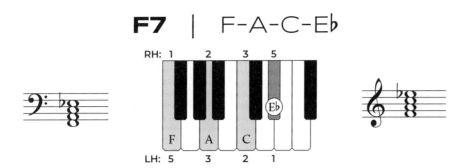

F7 | F–A–C–E♭

There are three further positions of this chord:

F7/A | A–C–E♭–F
(A on the bottom)

F7/C | C–E♭–F–A
(C on the bottom)

F7/E♭ | E♭–F–A–C
(E♭ on the bottom)

HOUND DOG
Words and Music by Jerry Leiber and Mike Stoller

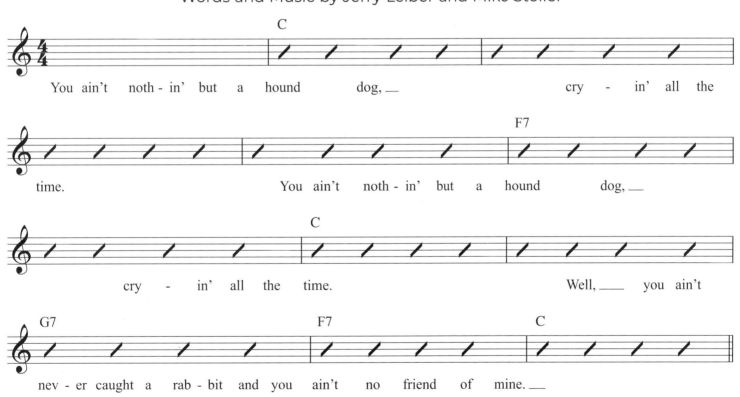

C

You ain't noth-in' but a hound dog, — cry-in' all the

time. You ain't noth-in' but a hound dog, —

C

cry - in' all the time. Well, — you ain't

G7   F7   C

nev - er caught a rab - bit and you ain't no friend of mine. —

D7 | D-F#-A-C

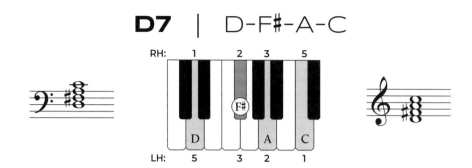

There are three further positions of this chord:

D7/F# | F#-A-C-D
(F# on the bottom)

D7/A | A-C-D-F#
(A on the bottom)

D7/C | C-D-F#-A
(C on the bottom)

FEELING GOOD
from THE ROAR OF THE GREASEPAINT - THE SMELL OF THE CROWD
Words and Music by Leslie Bricusse and Anthony Newley

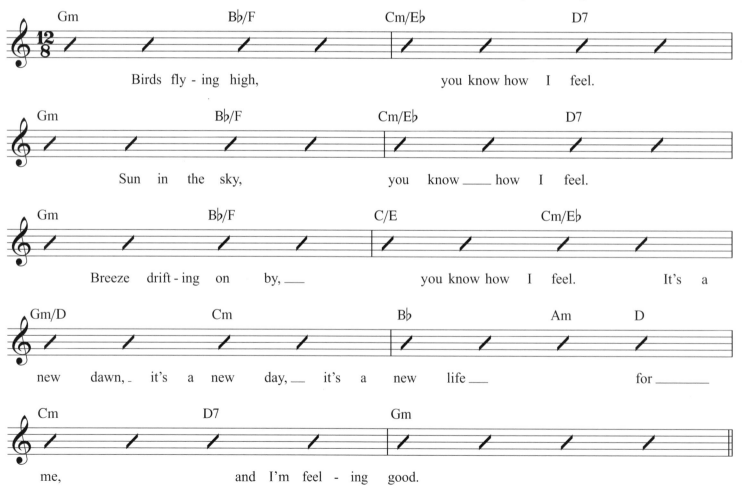

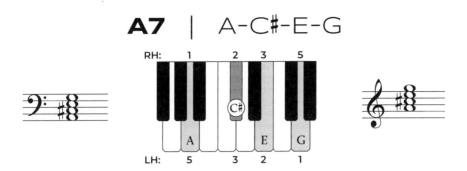

A7 | A-C#-E-G

There are three further positions of this chord:

A7/C# | C#-E-G-A
(C# on the bottom)

A7/E | E-G-A-C#
(E on the bottom)

A7/G | G-A-C#-E
(G on the bottom)

AMAZING GRACE
Words by John Newton
Traditional American Melody

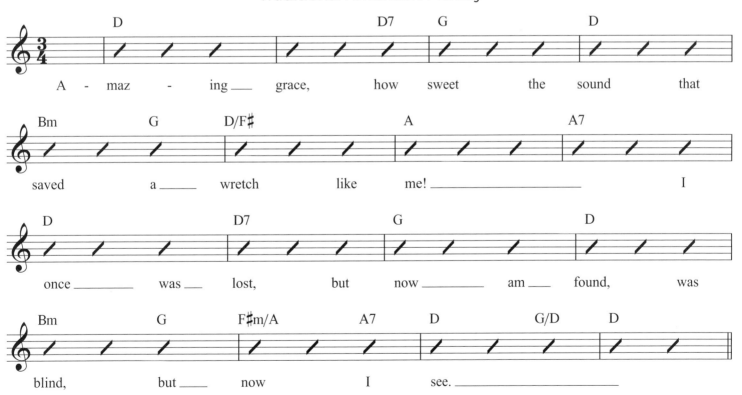

E7 | E–G♯–B–D

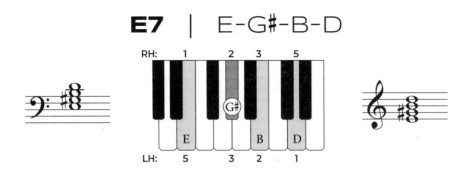

There are three further positions of this chord:

E7/G♯ | G♯–B–D–E
(G♯ on the bottom)

E7/B | B–D–E–G♯
(B on the bottom)

E7/D | D–E–G♯–B
(D on the bottom)

BLUE SUEDE SHOES
Words and Music by Carl Lee Perkins

B7 | B–D#–F#–A

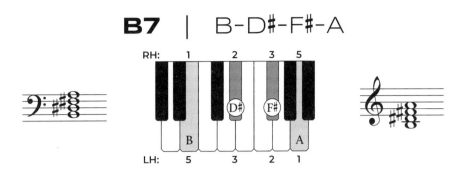

There are three further positions of this chord:

B7/D# | D#–F#–A–B
(D# on the bottom)

B7/F# | F#–A–B–D#
(F# on the bottom)

B7/A | A–B–D#–F#
(A on the bottom)

I SAW HER STANDING THERE
Words and Music by John Lennon and Paul McCartney

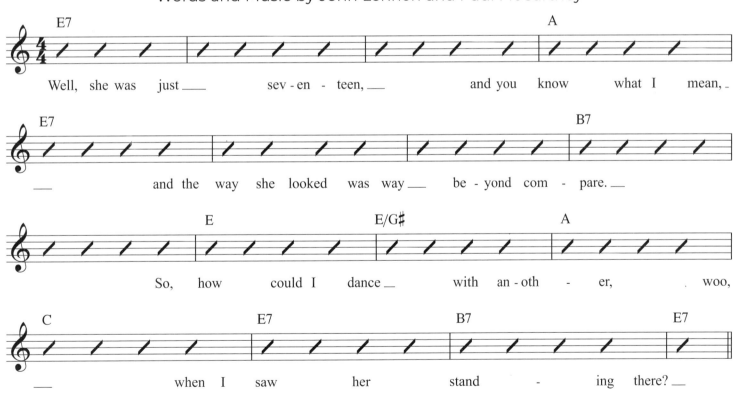

MAJOR SEVENTH CHORDS
C MAJOR SEVENTH

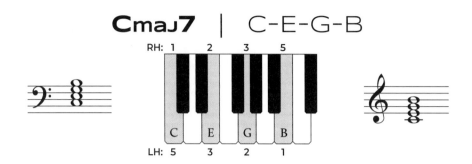

Cmaj7 | C-E-G-B

There are three further positions of this chord:

Cmaj7/E | E-G-B-C
(E on the bottom)

Cmaj7/G | G-B-C-E
(G on the bottom)

Cmaj7/B | B-C-E-G
(B on the bottom)

IMAGINE
Words and Music by John Lennon

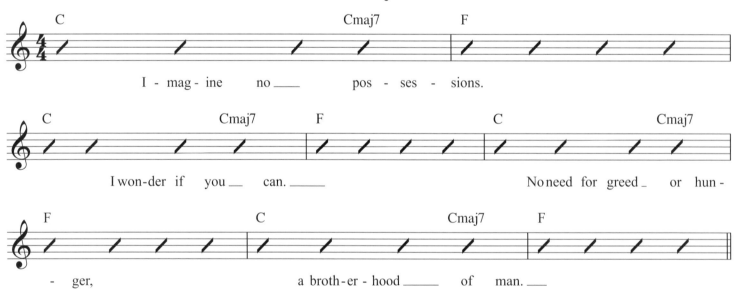

Fmaj7 | F-A-C-E

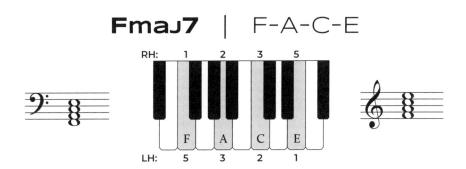

There are three further positions of this chord:

Fmaj7/A | A-C-E-F
(A on the bottom)

Fmaj7/C | C-E-F-A
(C on the bottom)

Fmaj7/E | E-F-A-C
(E on the bottom)

CALIFORNICATION
Words and Music by Anthony Kiedis, Flea, John Frusciante and Chad Smith

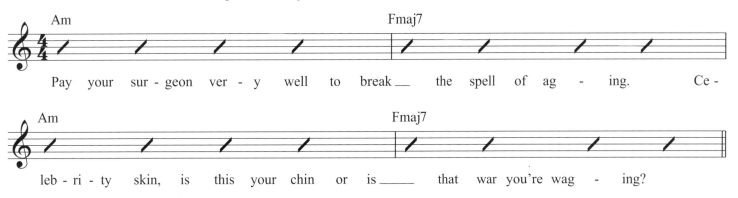

Pay your sur-geon ver-y well to break __ the spell of ag - ing. Ce-

leb-ri-ty skin, is this your chin or is ____ that war you're wag - ing?

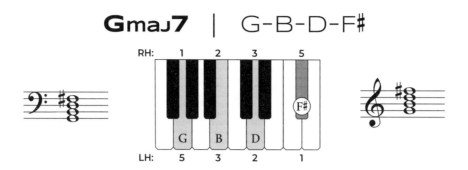

Gmaj7 | G-B-D-F#

There are three further positions of this chord:

Gmaj7/B | B-D-F#-G
(B on the bottom)

Gmaj7/D | D-F#-G-B
(D on the bottom)

Gmaj7/F# | F#-G-B-D
(F# on the bottom)

OOO BABY BABY
Words and Music by William "Smokey" Robinson and Warren Moore

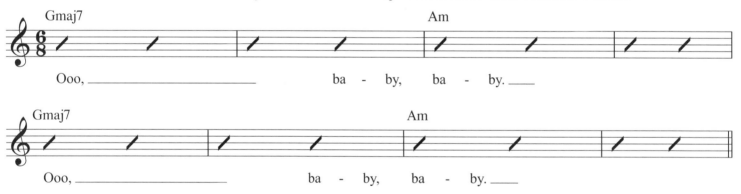

Amaj7 | A–C#–E–G#

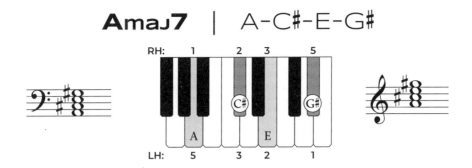

There are three further positions of this chord:

Amaj7/C# | C#–E–G#–A
(C# on the bottom)

Amaj7/E | E–G#–A–C#
(E on the bottom)

Amaj7/G# | G#–A–C#–E
(G# on the bottom)

BE OUR GUEST
from BEAUTY AND THE BEAST
Music by Alan Menken
Lyrics by Howard Ashman

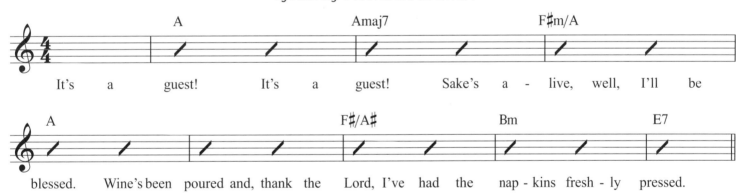

It's a guest! It's a guest! Sake's a-live, well, I'll be

blessed. Wine's been poured and, thank the Lord, I've had the nap-kins fresh-ly pressed.

Dmaj7 | D-F#-A-C#

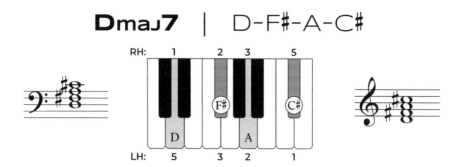

There are three further positions of this chord:

Dmaj7/F# | F#-A-C#-D
(F# on the bottom)

Dmaj7/A | A-C#-D-F#
(A on the bottom)

Dmaj7/C# | C#-D-F#-A
(C# on the bottom)

COFFEE
Words and Music by Beatrice Laus and Oscar Lang

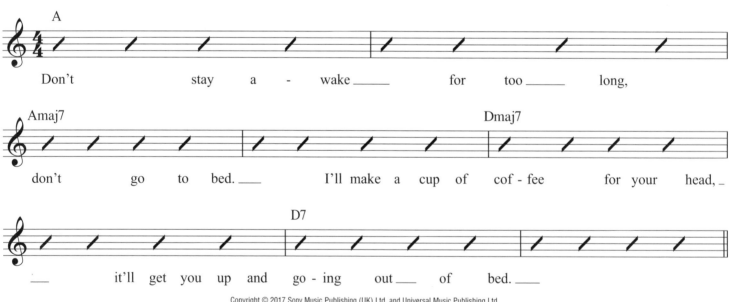

DIMINISHED SEVENTH CHORDS

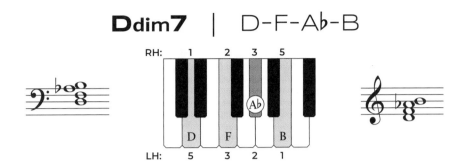

Ddim7 | D-F-A♭-B

There are three further positions of this chord:

Fdim7 | F-A♭-B-D
(F on the bottom)

A♭dim7 | A♭-B-D-F
(A♭ on the bottom)

Bdim7 | B-D-F-A♭
(B on the bottom)

THIS LOVE
Words and Music by Adam Levine and Jesse Carmichael

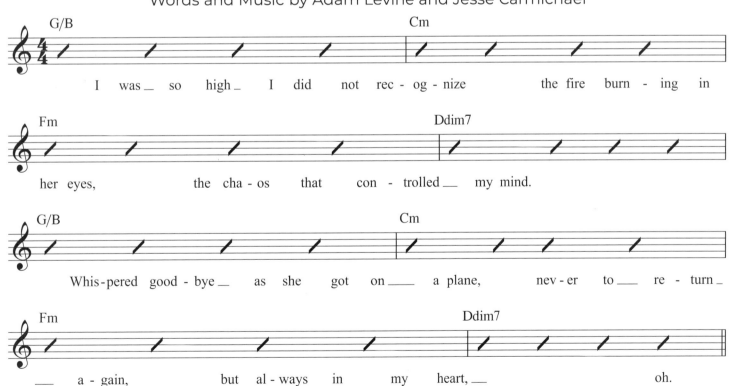

G/B — I was so high I did not rec-og-nize the fire burn-ing in

Cm — Fm — her eyes, the cha-os that con-trolled my mind.

Ddim7 — G/B — Whis-pered good-bye as she got on a plane, nev-er to re-turn

Cm — Fm — a-gain, but al-ways in my heart, oh.

Ddim7

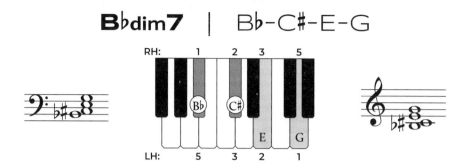

Bbdim7 | Bb-C#-E-G

There are three further positions of this chord:

C#dim7 | C#-E-G-Bb
(C# on the bottom)

Edim7 | E-G-Bb-C#
(E on the bottom)

Gdim7 | G-Bb-C#-E
(G on the bottom)

WE'RE ALL ALONE
Words and Music by Boz Scaggs

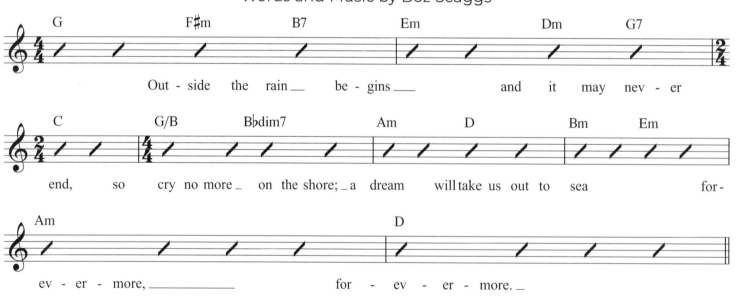

| G | F#m | B7 | Em | Dm | G7 |

Out-side the rain ___ be-gins ___ and it may nev-er

| C | G/B | Bbdim7 | Am | D | Bm | Em |

end, so cry no more ___ on the shore; ___ a dream will take us out to sea for-

| Am | | D | |

ev-er-more, _____ for-ev-er-more. ___

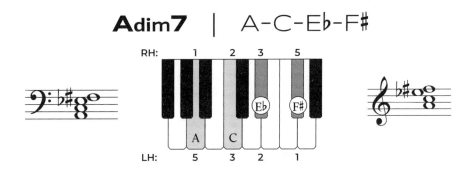

Adim**7** | A–C–E♭–F#

There are three further positions of this chord:

Cdim**7** | C–E♭–F#–A
(C on the bottom)

E♭dim**7** | E♭–F#–A–C
(E♭ on the bottom)

F#dim**7** | F#–A–C–E♭
(F# on the bottom)

BRIDGE OVER TROUBLED WATER
Words and Music by Paul Simon

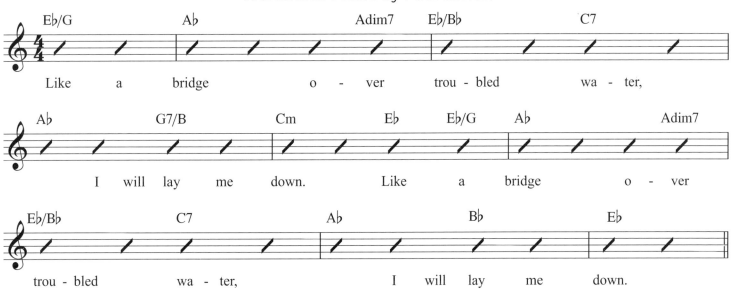

SUSPENDED FOURTH CHORDS

We'll interrupt our sevenths with one of the most popular chord types of them all: the **suspended fourth chord** (sus). To play this chord, you just take an ordinary major chord and move the middle note up a half step. Or you take an ordinary minor chord and move the middle note up one whole step.

D SUSPENDED FOURTH

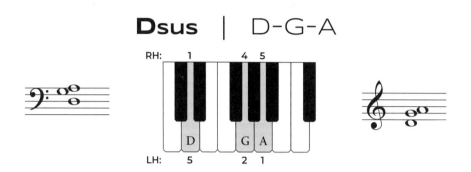

Dsus | D-G-A

There are two further positions of this chord:

Dsus/G | G-A-D
(G on the bottom)

Dsus/A | A-D-G
(A on the bottom)

CRAZY LITTLE THING CALLED LOVE
Words and Music by Freddie Mercury

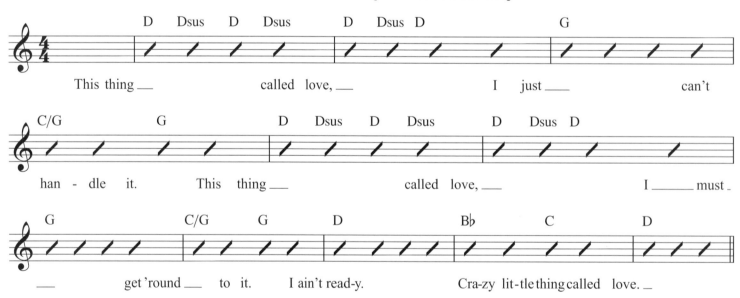

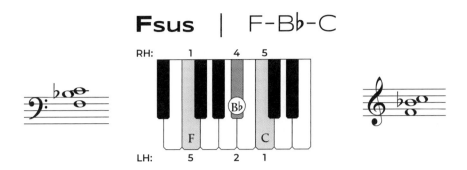

Fsus | F–B♭–C

There are two further positions of this chord:

Fsus/B♭ | B♭–C– F
(B♭ on the bottom)

Fsus/C | C–F–B♭
(C on the bottom)

FREE FALLIN'
Words and Music by Tom Petty and Jeff Lynne

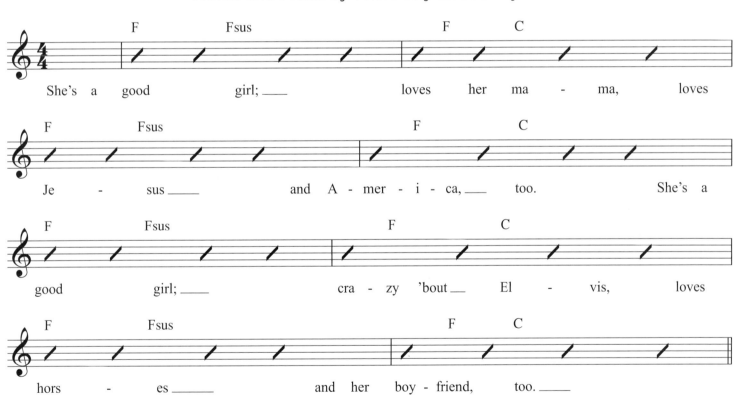

| | F | Fsus | | F | C |

She's a good girl; ___ loves her ma - ma, loves

| | F | Fsus | | F | C |

Je - sus ___ and A - mer - i - ca, ___ too. She's a

| | F | Fsus | | F | C |

good girl; ___ cra - zy 'bout ___ El - vis, loves

| | F | Fsus | | F | C |

hors - es ___ and her boy - friend, too. ___

Gsus | G-C-D

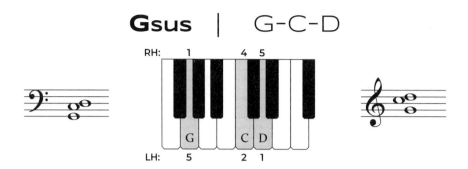

There are two further positions of this chord:

Gsus/C | C-D-G
(C on the bottom)

Gsus/D | D-G-C
(D on the bottom)

DON'T YOU WANT ME
Words and Music by Phil Oakey, Adrian Wright and Jo Callis

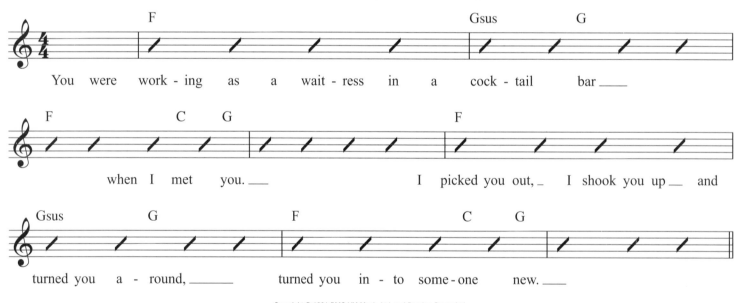

Asus | A-D-E

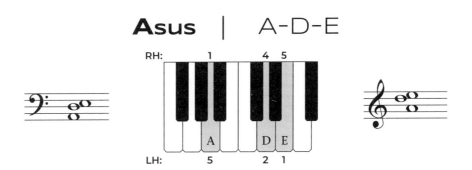

There are two further positions of this chord:

Asus/D | D-E-A
(D on the bottom)

Asus/E | E-A-D
(E on the bottom)

LIFE IN TECHNICOLOR II
Words and Music by Guy Berryman, Jon Buckland, Will Champion and Chris Martin

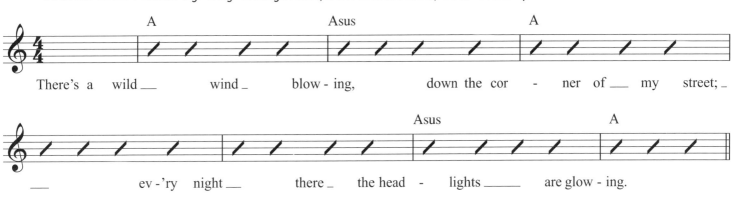

There's a wild __ wind _ blow - ing, down the cor - ner of __ my street; _ __ ev - 'ry night __ there _ the head - lights ____ are glow - ing.

Bsus | B-E-F♯

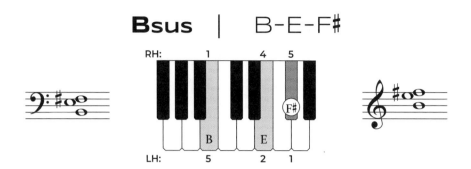

There are two further positions of this chord:

Bsus/E | E-F♯-B
(E on the bottom)

Bsus/F♯ | F♯-B-E
(F♯ on the bottom)

PINBALL WIZARD
Words and Music by Peter Townshend

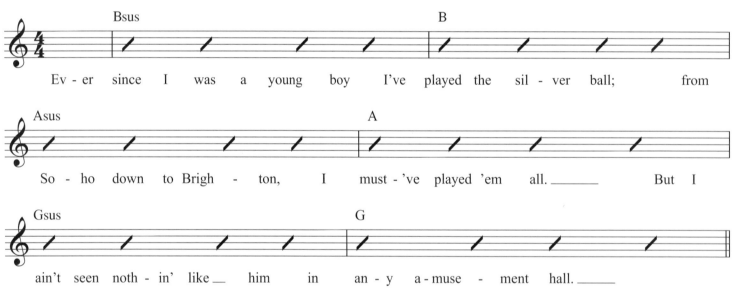

Bsus
Ev - er since I was a young boy I've played the sil - ver ball; from

Asus — A
So - ho down to Brigh - ton, I must - 've played 'em all._____ But I

Gsus — G
ain't seen noth - in' like __ him in an - y a - muse - ment hall._____

MINOR SEVENTH CHORDS
D MINOR SEVENTH

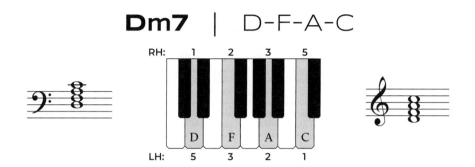

Dm7 | D-F-A-C

There are three further positions of this chord:

Dm7/F | F-A-C-D
(F on the bottom)

Dm7/A | A-C-D-F
(A on the bottom)

Dm7/C | C-D-F-A
(C on the bottom)

LIKE A ROLLING STONE
Words and Music by Bob Dylan

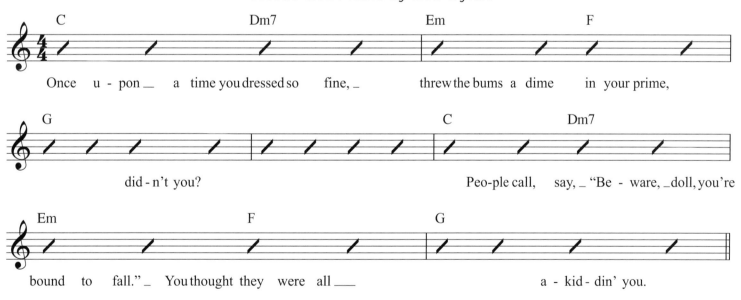

C   Dm7   Em   F

Once u - pon __ a time you dressed so fine, _ threw the bums a dime in your prime,

G   C   Dm7

did - n't you?   Peo-ple call, say, _ "Be - ware, _ doll, you're

Em   F   G

bound to fall." _ You thought they were all ___   a - kid - din' you.

Em7 | E-G-B-D

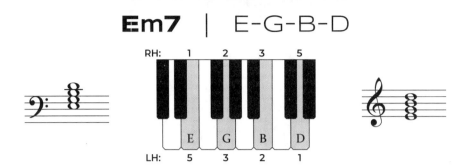

There are three further positions of this chord:

Em7/G | G-B-D-E
(G on the bottom)

Em7/B | B-D-E-G
(B on the bottom)

Em7/D | D-E-G-B
(D on the bottom)

ELEANOR RIGBY
Words and Music by John Lennon and Paul McCartney

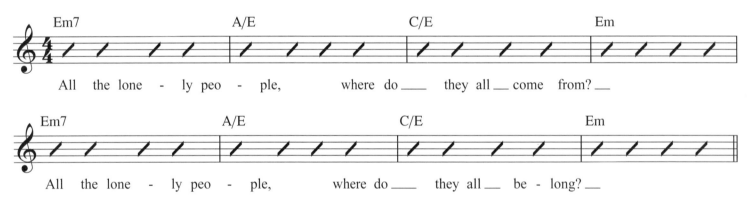

Cm7 | C-Eb-G-Bb

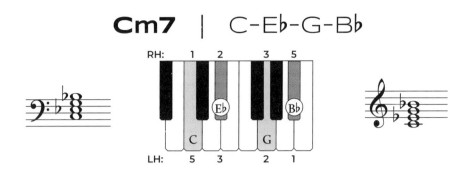

There are three further positions of this chord:

Cm7/Eb | Eb-G-Bb-C
(Eb on the bottom)

Cm7/G | G-Bb-C-Eb
(G on the bottom)

Cm7/Bb | Bb-C-Eb-G
(Bb on the bottom)

FUNKYTOWN
Words and Music by Steven Greenberg

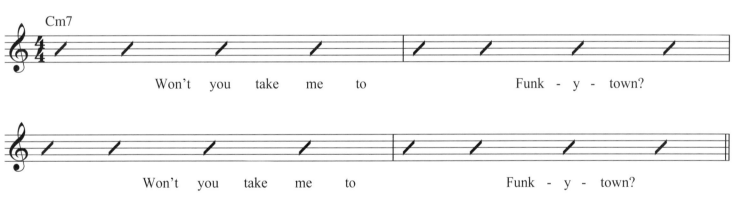

Bm7 | B-D-F♯-A

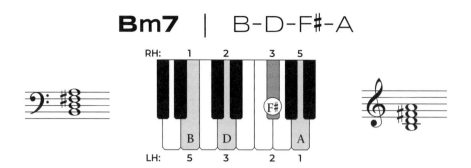

There are three further positions of this chord:

Bm7/D | D-F♯-A-B
(D on the bottom)

Bm7/F♯ | F♯-A-B-D
(F♯ on the bottom)

Bm7/A | A-B-D-F♯
(A on the bottom)

FALLIN'
Words and Music by Alicia Keys

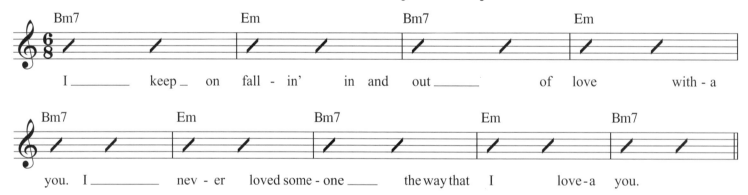

I _____ keep _ on fall - in' in and out _____ of love with - a

you. I _____ nev - er loved some - one _____ the way that I love-a you.

FIRST 50 SONGS
YOU SHOULD PLAY ON THE PIANO

*You've been taking lessons, you've got a few chords under your belt, and you're ready to buy a songbook.
Now what? Hal Leonard has the answers in its **First 50** series.*

*These books contain easy to intermediate arrangements with lyrics for must-know songs.
Each arrangement is simple and streamlined, yet still captures the essence of the tune.*

3-Chord Songs
00249666....................................$19.99

4-Chord Songs
00249562....................................$19.99

Acoustic Songs
00293416....................................$17.99

Baroque Pieces
00291453....................................$15.99

Blues Songs
00293318....................................$17.99

Broadway Songs
00150167....................................$17.99

Christmas Carols
00147216....................................$15.99

Christmas Songs
00172041....................................$15.99

Classic Rock
00195619....................................$17.99

Classical Pieces
00131436....................................$15.99

Country Songs
00150166....................................$16.99

Disney Songs
00274938....................................$22.99

Duets
00276571....................................$24.99

Early Rock Songs
00160570....................................$17.99

Folk Songs
00235867....................................$15.99

Fun Children's Songs
00355369....................................$16.99

Gospel Songs
00282526....................................$16.99

Hymns
00275199....................................$15.99

Jazz Classics
00363096....................................$16.99

Jazz Standards
00196269....................................$15.99

Kids' Songs
00196071....................................$15.99

Latin Songs
00248747....................................$17.99

Love Ballads
00457002....................................$19.99

Movie Songs
00150165....................................$17.99

Movie Themes
00278368....................................$17.99

Piano Solos
00365906....................................$17.99

Pop Ballads
00248987....................................$19.99

Pop Hits
00234374....................................$19.99

Popular Songs
00131140....................................$18.99

R&B Songs
00196028....................................$17.99

Relaxing Songs
00327506 ....$17.99

Rock Songs
00195619....................................$17.99

TV Themes
00294319....................................$15.99

Worship Songs
00287138....................................$19.99

HAL•LEONARD®
www.halleonard.com

*Prices, content and availability subject to
change without notice.*